100 QUEST[...] NSWERS

SEA

AND SEALIFE

Written by
Laura Wade

Edited by
Nicola Wright

zigzag

Laura Wade has worked for The Sea Life Centres for the past five years. Her position firstly as their Educational Services Manager, and now as Project Manager, has always involved her in exciting eductional wildlife developements. She is a trained natural history illustrator and has also worked for the World Wildlife Fund, The Whale and Dolphin Conservation Society and as a keeper for London Zoo. Her assistant on this book, Sarah Bradbury, is a trained marine biologist and Educational Services Officer at The Sea Life Centres.

ZIGZAG PUBLISHING LTD

Published by Zigzag Publishing Ltd, The Barn, Randolph's Farm, Brighton Road, Hurstpierpoint, West Sussex BN6 9EL, England

Series concept: Tony Potter
Designed by: Juan Hayward & Deborah Chadwick
Illustrated by: Peter Bull, Mainline Design, John Yates, Justine Peek, Rod Ferring, Janos Marffy, Michael Saunders, Peter Dennis
Cover design: Nicky Chapman
Cover illustration: Roger Stewart
Production: Zoë Fawcett

Colour separations: Sussex Repro, England
Printed by: Proost, Belgium

First published in 1995 by Zigzag Publishing Ltd

UK ISBN 1 85993 170 7
10 9 8 7 6 5 4 3 2 1

Contents

About this book

This book answers all your questions about the sea and sealife. You can find out about wierd and wonderful creatures living in the depths of the oceans and amongst the colourful coral reefs. Discover too what makes waves and if mermaids really exist.

Have you ever wondered how the sea was first formed, what causes the tides to rise and fall, or which is the deepest ocean and how it is explored? These questions and many more are answered by our sea experts.

You can also learn how the first sailor's navigated, the many ways people enjoy the sea today and why we must look after it.

When the sea was first formed it was hot, only a few degrees below boiling point, and as acidic as lemon juice!

What do we know about the sea?

The sea covers two thirds of the Earth and contains 97 per cent of all its water. As well as being the home of millions of fascinating creatures, humans rely on it for food, energy and fun.

Q What is the sea made of?

A The sea is made of salt water that contains every natural element known on Earth - altogether more than 100! If you dissolved a teaspoon of table salt in a glass of water, this would show you how salty the sea is. Sodium and chlorine, the main components of table salt, make up 85 per cent of the dissolved salts in sea water.

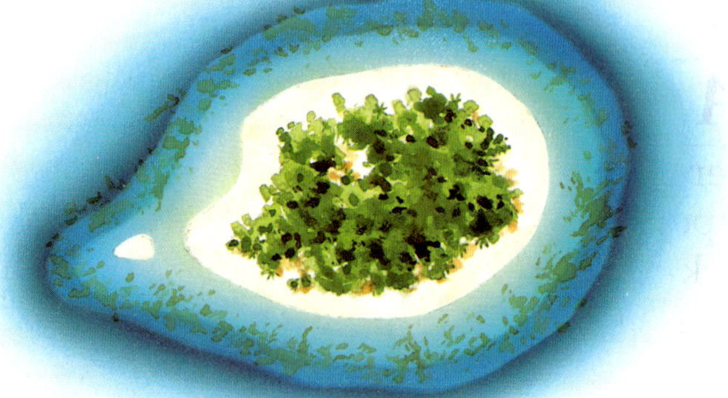

Sea water also contains calcium, magnesium and even traces of arsenic and gold!

Q Why is the sea blue?

A The sea is blue because it reflects the colour of the sky. When a cloud is overhead you can see it cast a shadow on the sea. The colour can also depend on how deep the water is. From above shallow water with sand on the seabed tends to look paler blue than deeper water with dark seaweed on the bottom. Weather conditions can also change the look of the sea. It can look dark grey in a storm.

Q Can sound travel through sea water?

A Yes. However, sound travels through sea water 4.5 times faster than it does through air. Because of this it is hard to tell what direction sound is coming from underwater as it seems to reach both ears at the same time.

The sea is a layer of water with an average depth of 2.3 miles on the surface of a sphere 800 miles wide.

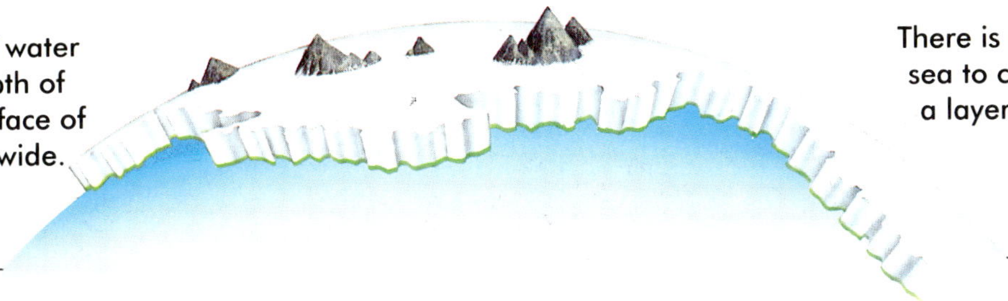

There is enough salt in the sea to cover the land with a layer 153 metres thick.

Q How was the sea first formed?

A Although they cannot be sure, scientists believe that the oceans were formed by massive clouds of water vapour rising from volcanoes and hot rocks on the Earth's surface not long after it was formed. As the surface cooled, the water vapour turned to rain which fell and fell, gradually filling up dips in the Earth's surface and taking with it any mineral salts on the land... and so forming the salt water oceans.

Q Where does sea water come from?

A Very little new water is ever made on Earth. It is just the same supply used over and over again. As the Sun heats up the sea, millions of litres of water rise up into the air as invisible water vapour. Clouds form as the water vapour cools, then as they drift over the land it rains or snows. Rivers collect the water and carry it straight back into the sea, and the whole process begins again. This is called the water cycle.

Q Can light travel through sea water?

A Sunlight is made up of the same colours you can see in a rainbow, starting with red and ending in violet. Each colour can only travel to a certain depth in sea water. For instance, red light fades out first at around five metres, whereas violet light can go as deep as 75 metres. Brightly coloured fish look dull if you see them deep down.

The hottest sea water is in the Persian Gulf. In summer the surface temperature can reach 35.6°C!

What is an ocean?

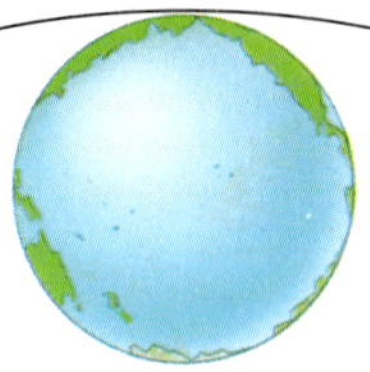

An ocean is a large body of water which is joined to other oceans and seas. Together they form one big stretch of water that flows continually around the world.

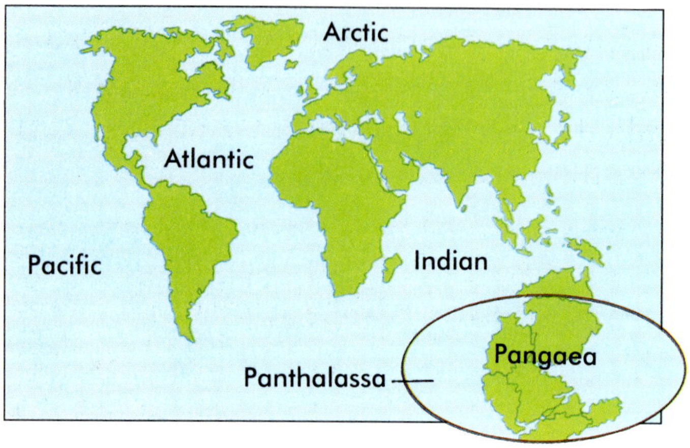

Q Which is the deepest ocean?

A The Pacific Ocean is the deepest as well as the largest. The deepest point in the ocean, and on Earth, is Marianas Trench, at 11,034 metres. Mount Everest, the highest mountain on Earth at 8,848 metres, could be sunk without trace into it. If a boat were to drop a 1 kg steel anchor over the side it would take over an hour to reach the bottom of the trench!

Q How many oceans are there?

A Today there are four recognised oceans. They are the Pacific, the Atlantic, the Indian and the Arctic. About 170 million years ago all the continents formed one piece of land called Pangaea. Surrounding it was one vast ocean called Panthalassa. As Pangaea slowly split into today's seven continents, Panthalassa became the four oceans.

Q What is the difference between an ocean and a sea?

A Oceans are bigger than seas. Some seas are parts of oceans, such as the Arabian Sea in the Indian Ocean. Other seas are enclosed by land, such as the Caspian Sea in Asia. All the oceans together are often just called 'the sea'.

Fossilised sea shells found on Mount Everest show that the Himalayas were once part of the sea floor. Changes in the Earth's crust pushed them up into the air about 40 million years ago.

Only one ninth of an iceberg is ever visible above the sea's surface.

Q Which is the largest ocean?

A The Pacific is the largest ocean, covering one third of the Earth. At its widest point, the Pacific measures 17,700 km, stretching nearly halfway round the world!

Q Which is the coldest ocean?

A The Arctic is the coldest ocean as well as the smallest. For most of the year it is frozen solid. In some places the ice measures up to 1.5 km thick! The Arctic Ocean is dotted with thousands of icebergs, with up to 15,000 new ones being formed each year!

Q In which ocean is the saltiest sea?

A The Red Sea in the Indian Ocean has the saltiest sea water in the world. Part of it, known as the Dead Sea, is famous for people being able to float on its surface with no effort at all. It is called the Dead Sea because nothing can live in the salty water.

Q Which is the smallest ocean?

A The Arctic Ocean is the smallest ocean, covering an area of 12,257,000 sq km.

Q Which is the warmest ocean?

A The Indian Ocean holds the record for being the warmest ocean. The temperature of the surface water can reach 35.6°C! It is the third largest ocean covering an area of 73,600,000 sq km.

The greatest tides occur in the Bay of Fundy in Canada, where they can rise to over 15 metres high.

What are currents and tides?

The waters of the world's oceans and seas are continually flowing. They are moved by the wind, waves, tides and currents.

Q What is a current?

A Currents are bodies of water that always flow in the same direction. They are driven mainly by the wind.

Q What is the Gulf Stream?

A The Gulf Stream is one of the strongest, warmest and saltiest currents. It runs along the east coast of the USA, separating the warm, salty Sargasso Sea from the cold, less salty inshore water.

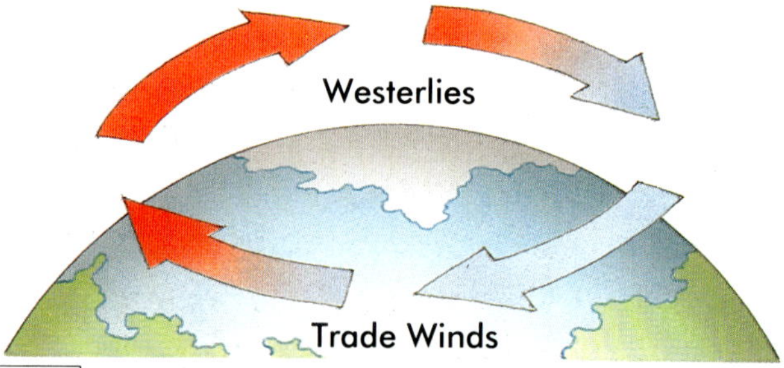

Q What causes a current?

A Wind-driven currents are controlled by two types of winds. These are called the Westerlies (that blow from west to east), and the Trade Winds (that blow from east to west). These winds force the warm water at the Equator out towards the cold water of the North Pole in a clockwise direction, and out towards the cold water of the South Pole in an anti-clockwise direction.

Q What are tides?

A Tides are the sea level rising and falling twice each day. You can see the tide is rising when the water covers the beach. When the water stops rising it is high tide. The water level then falls back until low tide is reached.

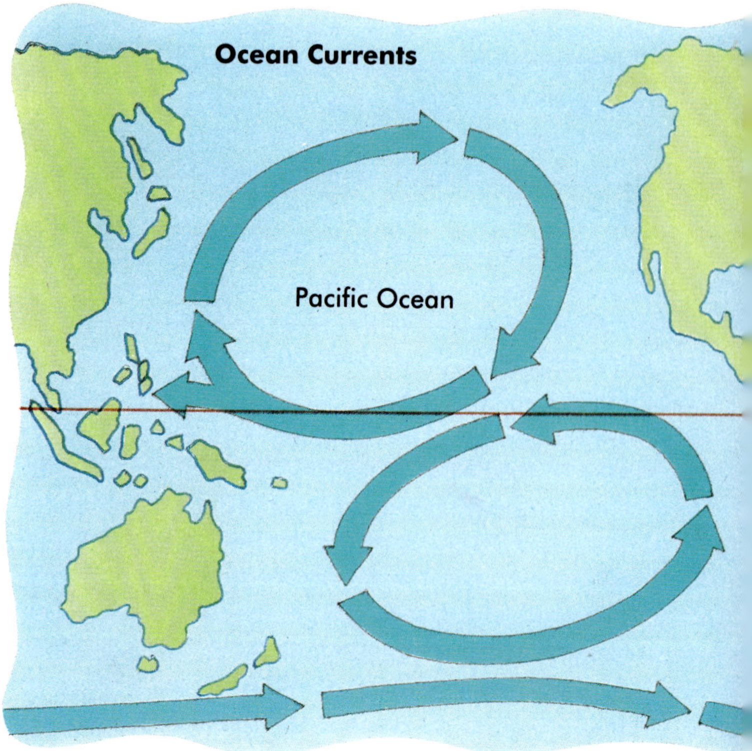

Warm currents may be as hot as 30°C, while cold currents may be as cold as -2°C.

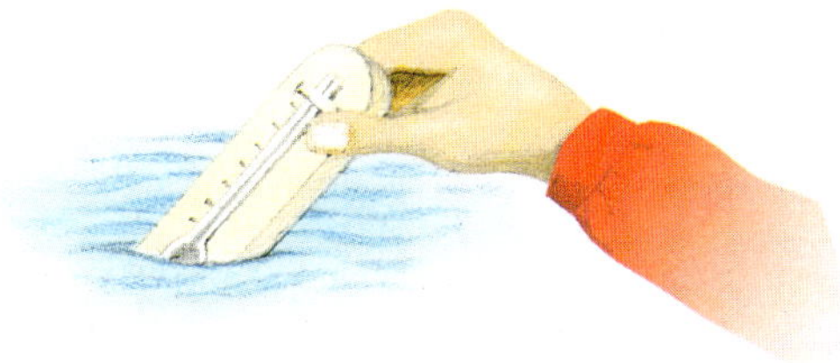

One drop of sea water may take 5000 years to travel through all the world's oceans.

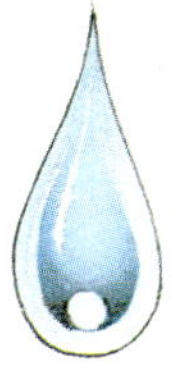

Q **Are currents dangerous?**

A Yes. Underwater sea currents cause many deaths each year. Bathers swim out to areas which look calm on the surface, but then they are pulled away from or along the shore by strong currents underneath. Once trapped in the pull of a current, a swimmer can become exhausted and even drown.

Q **What causes high and low tides?**

A Tides are caused by the Moon's gravity pulling the Earth's oceans into two bulges, one facing the Moon and another on the other side of the planet. As the Moon travels around the Earth, it drags these bulges of water with it. As the bulge hits the land, the water piles up, creating a high tide. Between the bulges the water is lower, creating a low tide.

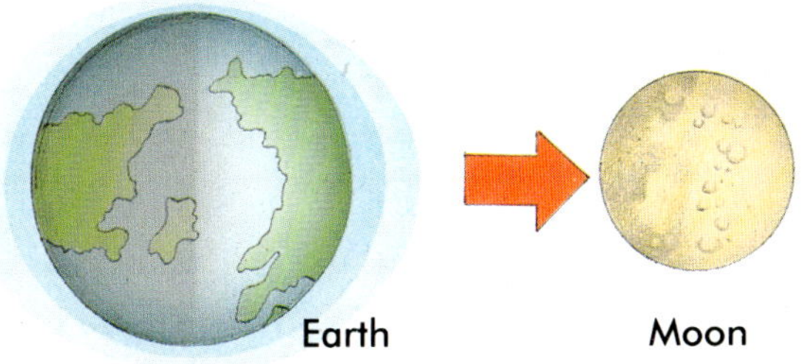

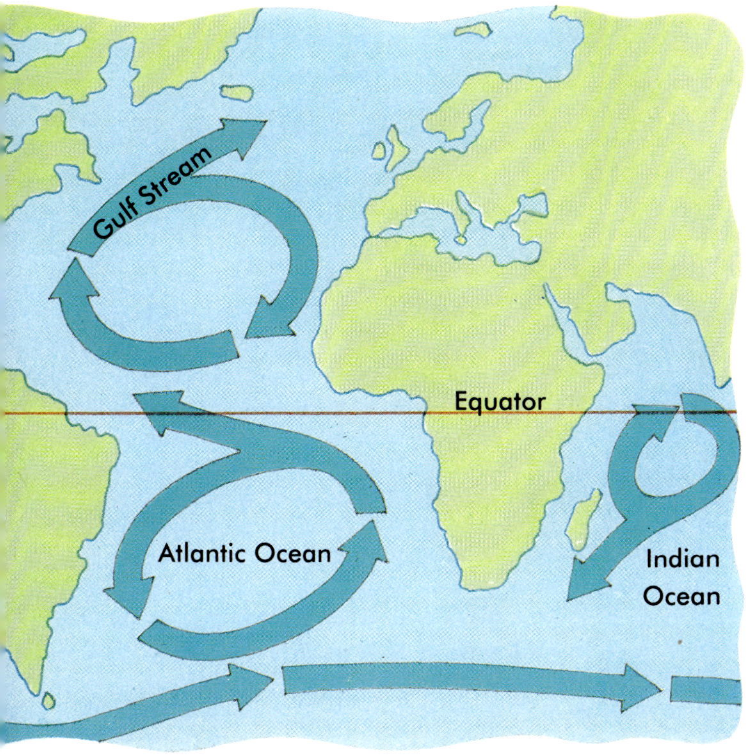

Q **What causes spring and neap tides?**

A When the Moon is lined up with the Sun, they pull together on the same point of the Earth's surface. This big pull causes a massive bulge which makes the high tides very high and the low tides very low. This is known as a spring tide. When the Moon has moved to a right angle with the Sun, their pull evens out and so there is no bulge.

During this time there is very little difference between low and high tide. This is called a neap tide. A spring and a neap tide occur twice a month.

The largest tsunami ever recorded was off the Japanese coast in 1971. It was 85 metres high!

How are waves formed?

Waves come in all shapes and sizes, from small and rippling to huge and crashing. Some can even capsize a ship.

Q What is a wave?

A A wave is a mass of tiny water particles going round in a circular movement. Each water droplet ends up exactly where it began in the circle.

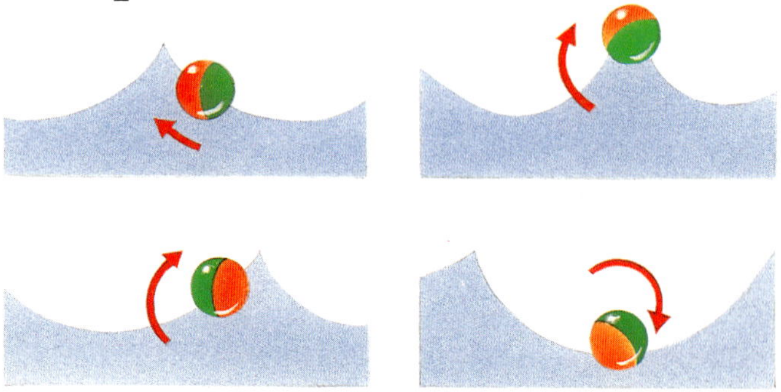

Q What makes waves?

A Waves are made by the wind blowing across the surface of the water. The wind pushes the water upwards and then gravity pulls it back down again. So the stronger the wind and the longer it blows, the bigger the waves it creates.

Q What are tidal waves or tsunamis?

A They are giant waves caused by earthquakes and volcanic eruptions under the sea. They explode on the shore causing great damage, and can even drown whole islands.

Q How do you measure a wave?

A To see how big a wave is, you have to measure from its crest (the highest point of the wave) to its trough (the lowest point of the wave).

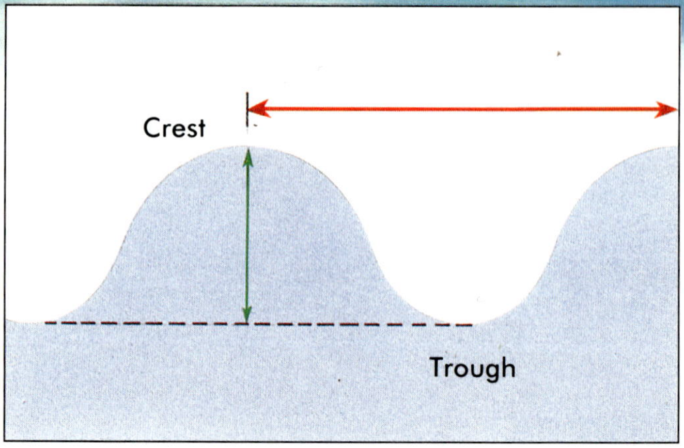

In June 1968, the tanker World Glory was broken in two by a series of 30 metre-high waves.

The white foam that forms on the crests of waves is often called 'white horses'.

Q Are waves dangerous?

A Some waves can be very dangerous, especially in storms. They can wreck ships out at sea. Freak waves sometimes rise up and snatch people from the shore, dragging them into the sea. Surfers often try to ride extremely high waves, which can crush and drown them if they fall off their surf boards.

Q What height can waves reach?

A Waves can reach enormous heights. The highest natural wave ever recorded was 34 metres, seen from *USS Ramapo* during a storm in the Pacific Ocean in 1933. That is over 20 times taller than an average person!

Q What are waterspouts?

A Waterspouts are enormous columns of water drawn up by the wind quite suddenly. In the Gulf of Mexico, winds blowing at up to 965 km/h turn into tornadoes or whirlwinds as they come off the land and whip up massive waterspouts. Some may be 10 metres thick and 120 metres high!

Not all beaches have yellow sand. Hawaiin beaches have black sand, formed from volcanic lava.

What is on the seashore?

The seashore is where the land meets the sea. Some seashores have flat beaches, while others have steep cliffs. They are always busy with all kinds of wildlife.

Q How are beaches made?

A Rocks are constantly broken off from the land by the sea and worn down into smaller and smaller pieces, making pebbles or sand. These are then dropped off along the shore by waves and a beach is gradually formed. Sand is also brought from inland by rivers flowing into the sea.

Q What lives under the sand on a beach?

A Sandy beaches may not seem to have many creatures living on them at first glance. But if you look carefully you will see signs of life. Tiny holes, hollows and piles of coiled sand give away the hiding places of bristle worms, rag worms, cockles and burrowing starfish and crabs. Under the sand they are protected from the Sun, predators and tides.

Q How does the sea shape the seashore?

A Waves are constantly wearing away the shore and changing its shape. It hollows out caves and arches in cliffs.

Q What plants do you find on the seashore?

A Algae and seaweed are the only plants you find on the seashore. Most plants do not like salt water and sea breezes.

Like rocks, seaweeds provide a cool hiding place for creatures while they wait for the tide to come in. Gently turn clumps of seaweed over and see what is hiding underneath!

The Bermuda Islands have pale pink beaches. The sand is made from tiny pieces of red shell.

The dazzling white beaches of Barbados are made from tiny pieces of white shell.

Q What is a strandline?

A When the tide comes in it leaves behind a long line of debris at its edge. This is called a strandline. People go beachcombing along strandlines, searching for pretty seashells, mermaid's purses (shark's egg cases), crab shells, cuttlefish bones, driftwood and even useful rubbish.

Q What animals like beaches?

A Seabirds, such as gulls, feed on dead fish and crabs washed up on the strandline. Wading birds use their long beaks for finding worms in the sand. Huge colonies of seals gather on beaches at certain times of the year to mate.

Q What might you find in a rock pool?

A Water is trapped in the hollows of rocks (worn out of them by the sea) when the tide goes out, forming rock pools. They provide a home for many creatures. Starfish, anemones, limpets, periwinkles and mussels cling to the rocks, while shrimps, crabs and different types of fish shelter underneath them.

Many flatfish can change their skin colour and pattern to match whatever surface they rest on.

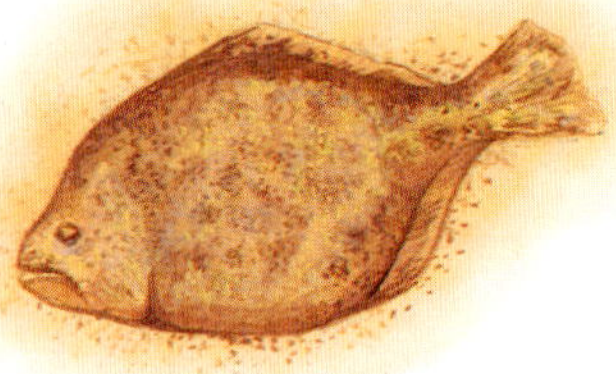

What lives in the sea?

Life on Earth started in the sea over 3,500 million years ago. At one time almost all life existed there. Today, there is still a bigger variety of animal and plant life in the sea than on land.

Q What is plankton?

A Plankton is a soup of millions of tiny plants known as phytoplankton and minute animals known as zooplankton, that drift near the surface of the water. It is eaten by many sea creatures including baleen whales. They have huge comb-like sieves hanging down from the roofs of their mouths which trap the plankton.

Q What is the biggest creature in the sea?

A The blue whale weighs 150 tonnes, and can measure 33 metres long. It is harmless though, feeding only on tiny zooplankton called krill. It needs to sieve four tonnes of krill a day to survive!

Q How many species of fish are there?

A So far more than 21,000 species of fish have been recorded. The largest fish is the whale shark, measuring 18 metres long. The smallest fish is the dwarf goby, measuring less than 10 mm long - it will fit on the end of a human fingernail!

Dolphins are very friendly creatures. They often swim alongside ships for miles, leaping out of the water.

Whales sing to each other underwater. Their eerie wails can be heard miles away.

Q What mammals live in the sea?

A Seals, whales and dolphins are all sea mammals. Like mammals on land they are warm blooded, have a backbone and hair, breathe air and take care of their young after they are born.

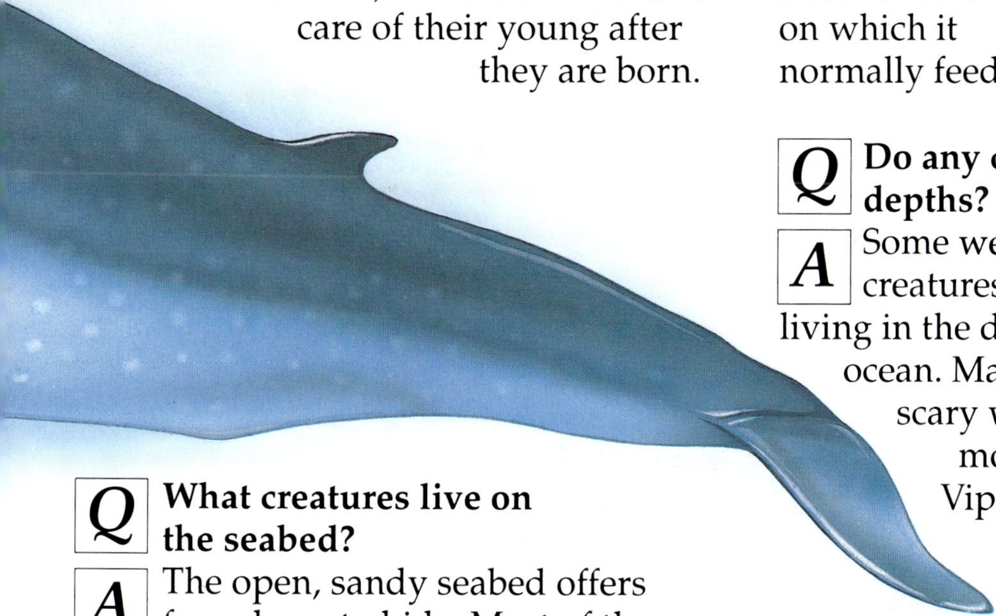

Q What is the most feared animal in the sea?

A Humans have a fear of sharks, especially the great white shark. However, many sharks are harmless. The great white is unlikely to attack a human unless provoked or if it mistakes a swimmer for a seal or turtle on which it normally feeds.

Q Do any creatures live in the ocean depths?

A Some weird and wonderful creatures have been discovered living in the darkest depths of the ocean. Many of them are extremely scary with little eyes, huge mouths and fang-like teeth. Viper fish, gulper eels and the deep sea angler fish all look like they are from a horror film!

Q What creatures live on the seabed?

A The open, sandy seabed offers few places to hide. Most of the creatures that live there have flat bodies and are well camouflaged so they can lie hidden from predators and prey. Rays, plaice and other flatfish live on the seabed.

In 1969 four scientists lived in a special home, called Tektite, on the seabed for 60 days!

What is in the ocean depths?

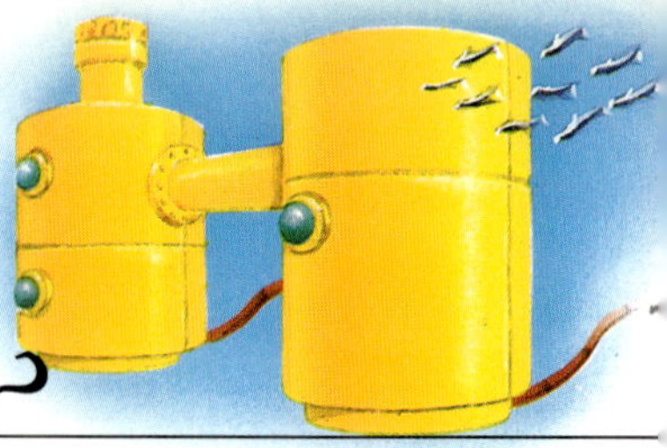

Humans have only been able to explore the depths of the oceans in the last century. Expensive, highly technical equipment is needed for us to breathe and cope with the extreme cold and pressure.

Q How do we explore the ocean depths?

A We need underwater crafts like submersibles, submarines and bathyscaphes. These are all specially designed to protect the crew from high pressure underwater and enables them to work for fairly long periods without returning to the surface. Small submersibles can travel down to 1,200 metres and stay there for 48 hours, while a large nuclear submarine can be submerged for months!

Q How do we know how deep the sea is?

A We can measure the depth of the sea with an echo sounder. Sound waves are bounced off the seabed back to an echo sounder in a boat. Scientists can work out the depth from how long it takes for the sound waves to travel back.

Q How deep has a submersible travelled beneath the sea?

A On 23 January 1960, a bathyscaphe called *Trieste* reached the bottom of the Marianas Trench, the deepest part of the ocean. It took them 4 hours and 48 minutes to travel 11,034 metres.

A diver coming up too quickly from the deep can get 'the bends'. Nitrogen gas bubbles enter the blood causing extreme pain.

Deep sea angler fish have a glowing light dangling in front of their mouths to attract prey.

Q Is there light in the ocean depths?

A No. No light at all penetrates deeper than 1,000 metres. Most light filters out at 10 metres. Not only does the sea get darker the deeper you go, but it also gets colder. At 4,000 metres deep it is as cold as the inside of a fridge!

Q How do deep sea creatures see?

A Some creatures which live in the dark ocean depths produce their own light called bioluminescence. This light helps them to see where they are going, trap prey and find a mate in the dark. Flashlight fish have two light organs under each eye, made up of billions of microscopic glowing bacteria.

Q Are there seaquakes?

A Yes. Many seaquakes happen in the 'Ring of Fire' around the Pacific Ocean. Most are never felt above or even near the surface.

Q Are there underwater mountains?

A Yes. Some mountains underwater are so huge their peaks rise out above the surface. The highest mountain on Earth is not Mount Everest, but Mount Kea in the Pacific Ocean. It is a volcanic mountain which rises a staggering 10,203 metres off the sea floor.

Q What is on the ocean floor?

A When a marine animal or plant dies it is either eaten or its body drifts down to the seabed to decay. About 75 per cent of the deep ocean floor is covered in a thick gunge made up from the decaying bodies of plants and animals and mud.

Thousands of tiny islands in the Pacific Ocean are made entirely of coral.

What is a coral reef?

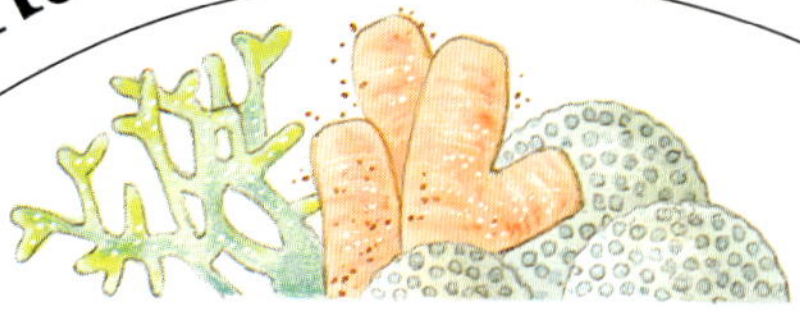

Coral reefs are as important in the sea as rainforests are on the land. They provide shelter and feeding grounds for fish and other sea creatures and protect coastlines. As a major tourist attraction coral reefs also provide a large income for some countries.

Q How is a coral reef made?

Polyp

A Coral reefs are built by millions of tiny animals called polyps. Each animal grows a tough, chalky outer skeleton to protect its soft body. When polyps die, these tough outer cases build up on top of one another over the centuries forming the framework of massive coral reefs.

Q What lives in a coral reef?

A The rich food supply carried in the water surrounding coral reefs, plus the shelter that the reefs offer, attracts hundreds of colourful and exotic sea creatures. Parrot fish, angel fish, lion fish, butterfly fish and stone fish can be seen swimming around in the water. Anemones, starfish, sea slugs and clams cling to the coral.

Q What are some of the weirdest creatures living in coral reefs?

A Puffer fish blow themselves up like balloons to defend themselves. Some fish, like sea dragons, have flaps of skin to disguise themselves amongst rocks and seaweed.

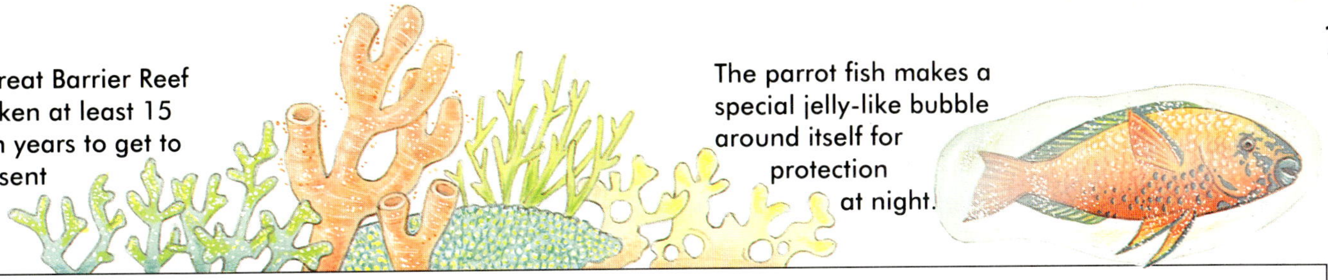

Q **Where are corals found?**

A Big, colourful coral reefs are found only in tropical and semi-tropical seas, such as the Red Sea. However, some small, non-reef-building corals can be found in colder waters, like cup corals. Coral reefs grow best at 7-20 metres below the surface of the sea, in clean water at 25-29°C.

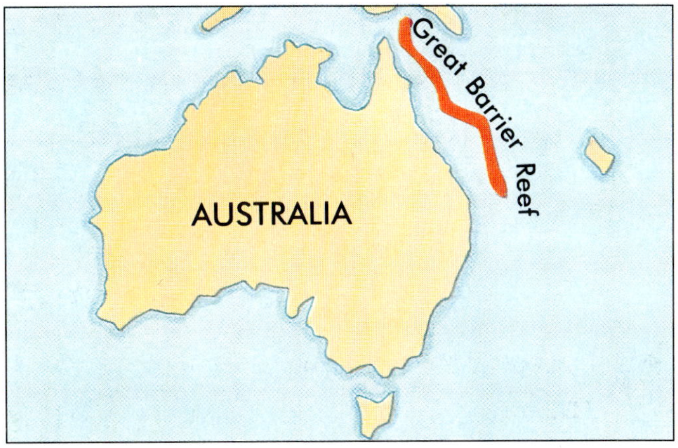

Q **What destroys coral reefs?**

A Some creatures actually eat the coral. Parrot fish break off lumps of coral with their sharp beaks, whilst the crown of thorns starfish can eat 300-400 sq cms of coral in one day! The reefs are also being destroyed by people.

Q **Which is the largest coral reef?**

A The Great Barrier Reef off the coast of Queensland in Australia is the largest coral reef in the world. It stretches for 2,027 km and covers an area of 207,000 sq km. The reef is so huge it can even be seen from the Moon!

Q **Which coral reef creatures can be dangerous?**

A Most sea creatures are not dangerous unless frightened. Six-foot moray eels lurk under rocks, waiting to lunge out at their prey. Sting rays have poisonous spines on the end of their long, whip-like tails. People have died after standing on the highly poisonous stone fish which looks like the rough surface of coral.

The fastest racing power boats can travel at speeds of over 230 km per hour.

How do we travel by sea?

Before the invention of the aeroplane, the only way to get to another country was by land or sea. The first boats were called 'dug outs', made from hollowed-out tree trunks. The range of sea vessels made today make travelling by sea much easier, faster and safer.

Q What are the largest ships built today?

A Oil tankers are the largest type of ship built today. One of the biggest is called the *Jahre Viking*. It is 485.45 metres long and when fully loaded it weighs a massive 564,739 tonnes!

Q What is the fastest passenger sea vessel?

A The quickest way to travel by sea today is by hovercraft. It travels very fast over the surface of the water on a cushion of air. The SR.N4 passenger hovercraft crosses the English Channel at an average speed of 65 knots.

Q What is a knot?

A Speed at sea is measured in knots (one knot = 1.85 km per hour). The term comes from an old method used by sailors. A piece of wood was tied to a rope that had a knot tied in it every 14.4 metres. When the wood was thrown into the sea, it pulled the rope after it. By counting the knots dragged out in 28 seconds the ship's speed could be calculated.

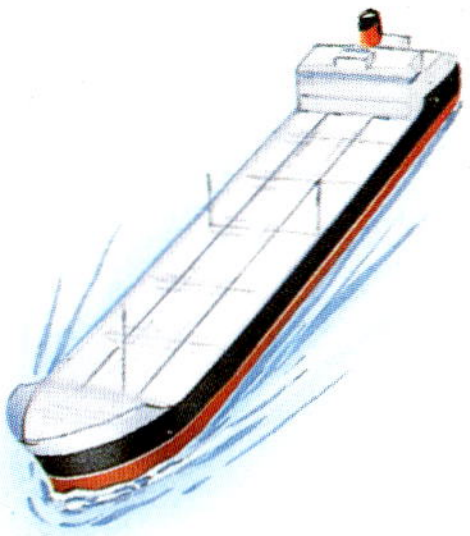

It can take a large oil tanker up to 6 km to stop at sea!

The earliest surviving 'dug out' was found in Holland and is believed to be around 8,500 years old.

Q How do sailors navigate today?

A Today navigation at sea is much easier and far more accurate than it used to be with the help of computers, radios, radar and satellite links. This modern technology helps to prevent collisions between ships, and allows a ship's crew to pinpoint their position.

Q How did the first sailors navigate?

A In early times sailors navigated by using the Sun, the Moon and the stars. They plotted the position of their ship using a special instrument called a sextant. This measured the distance between the Sun or the Moon above the horizon at various times of day or night.

Q How does a lighthouse work?

A Every year lighthouses around our coasts save ships from being wrecked on rocks. Today, a lighthouse beam is created by a huge, powerful electric lamp which sends a flash of light out to sea about every 15 seconds. Before the invention of electricity, lighthouses had oil lamps and large mirrors to reflect and increase the light. Before that they simply used firelight.

Q What do buoys do?

A Buoys are coloured metal floats which are anchored to the seabed. They warn ships of dangerous rocks, sandbanks or wrecks and mark the safe channels.

Icebergs are made of fresh water. They could be towed to countries suffering from drought and melted for drinking water.

How do we use the sea?

Ever since people inhabited the Earth, we have relied on it for many things. Modern technology means we can extract valuable resources, important to modern living.

Q Are there farms under the sea?

A Yes. Many countries breed shellfish and fish in special enclosures under the sea as it is easier to collect them and they can control the conditions to make them grow faster and bigger. The Japanese have underwater seaweed farms as they like to eat it. Salt farms trap and dry the salt in sea water and it is then cleaned.

Salt farm

Seaweed drying

Oyster farm

Lobster

Q Why are whales killed?

A Today only a few countries kill whales, and the numbers they are allowed to kill is restricted. However, the way in which they are killed is cruel and organisations like Greenpeace are trying to stop whaling completely. Many products contain whale including oil, pet foods, cosmetics, candles and fertilizers.

Q How is energy made from the waves?

A The tumbling motion of the waves is used to make electricity. Special giant rockers which float on the surface of the water are pushed up and down by the force of the waves. This pushes water through a shaft inside, which in turn drives a turbine, and so makes a constant source of electricity.

A large oil rig may produce enough oil in one day to fill 70,000 cars with petrol!

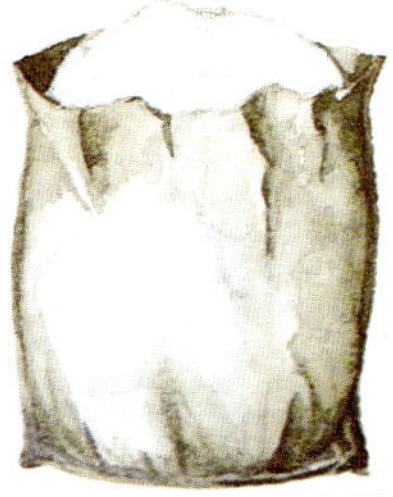

Six million tonnes of salt are taken from the sea each year for commercial use.

Q What sea creatures do we eat?

A Each year over 70 million tonnes of fish are caught in the oceans for food. Cockles, mussels, oysters, lobsters and crabs provide us with seafood.

Q How is energy made from the tides?

A Tidal power stations channel water through tunnels and past large blades. The force of the water coming in and going out turns the blades, which drive turbines, spinning a generator which produces electricity.

Q Can you drink sea water?

A You should avoid drinking sea because the salt and chemicals in it will make you sick. However, it can be drunk if the water is boiled and distilled and the salt evaporated.

Q How is oil extracted from the seabed?

A Once oil is found, it is extracted by drilling deep down into the seabed to make an oil well from which oil can be pumped. The oil is then transported away from the oil rig, either by pipelines to the shore or, if the rig is right out at sea, by huge oil tankers which can carry 500,000 tonnes of oil in one trip!

Q What other valuable resources come from the sea?

A Sand and gravel are extracted in huge amounts for commercial use. Shells and sponges are collected and sold. Diamonds are sucked up from the seabed off Southwest Africa. Pearls are collected from oysters. Gold has even been mined off the coasts of Alaska.

The furthest a sailing boat has ever sailed in a day is 462 miles.

How do we enjoy the sea?

For centuries, people all over the world have found pleasure in the sea, using it to swim, dive or fish in, sail or surf on, either for competitive sport or just for fun.

Q Who swam the longest ocean swim?

A The longest ocean swim was undertaken by Walter Poenisch in the Atlantic Ocean. In July 1978 he swam from Cuba to Florida in 34 hours and 15 minutes!

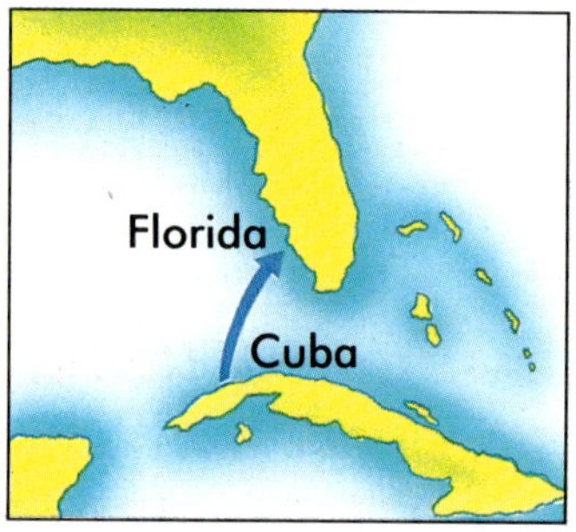

Q What is the record for swimming the English Channel?

A In 1978 Penny Dean swam the English Channel in 7 hours and 40 minutes from Dover in England to Cap Gris-Nez in France.

Q What is the quickest time for sailing around the world?

A It took Frenchman Bruno Peyron and his crew just 79 days 6 hours and 16 minutes to sail non-stop around the world. They completed this massive journey on 20 April 1993.

Q How deep is the deepest underwater dive?

A The record for an underwater breath-held dive stands at 107 metres, achieved by Angela Bandini on 3 October 1989. She was underwater for 2 minutes and 36 seconds! However, with the aid of SCUBA diving equipment, a dive of 133 metres has been made. In 1992 Theo Mavrostomos dived to a staggering 701 metres using SCUBA equipment filled with a special mixture of hydrogen, oxygen and helium.

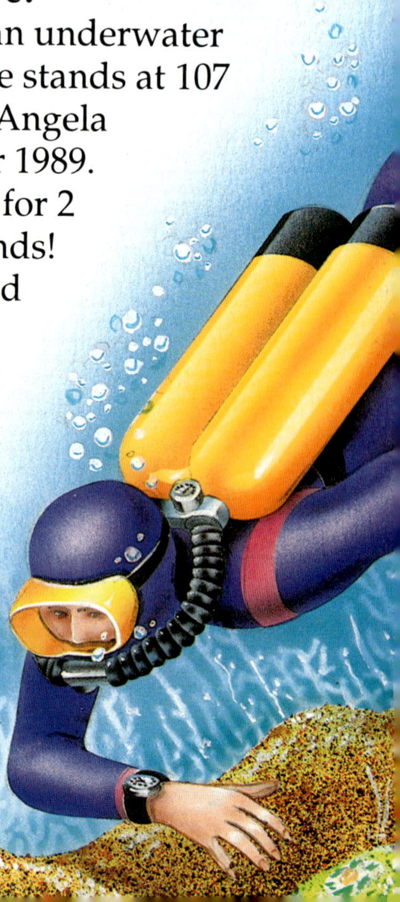

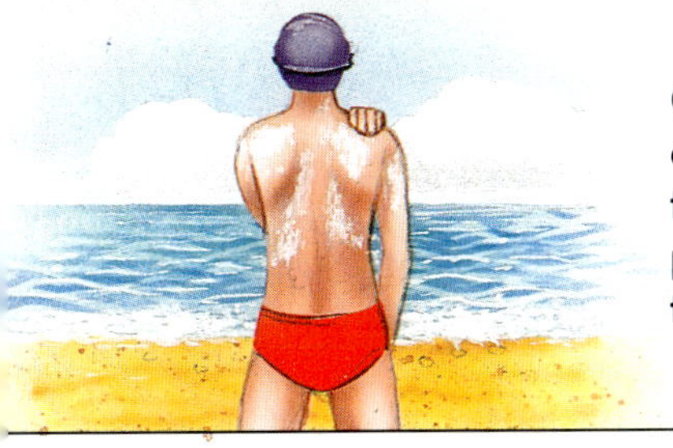

Channel swimmers cover themselves in thick grease to protect them against the cold water.

A record 100 water skiers were towed together for over a mile off the coast of Australia in 1986.

Q **Who were the first people to sail?**

A The Ancient Egyptians were the first people known to sail 5,000 years ago. Their sails were square and made out of reeds. Today some of the biggest sailing boats have as many as 30 sails and need about 200 people to raise and lower them.

Q **What is the highest wave surfed?**

A The highest wave ever ridden was a tsunami that struck Hawaii on 3 April 1868. To save his life, a Hawaiian named Holua rode this massive 165-metre wave. Good surfers regularly ride waves between 9 and 11 metres high off Waimea Bay in Hawaii.

Q **How fast is the fastest waterskier?**

A The fastest record for waterskiing is held by Christopher Massey. On 6 March 1983 he travelled at 230.26 km per hour.

Even today, some people pay homage to the sea god Neptune when they cross the Equator for the first time.

What sea legends are there?

In the 15th Century people believed that the Earth was flat and that if you sailed too far from land you would fall off the edge!

Many unexplained mysteries surround the sea. Sailors returning from long jouneys often told stories of huge sea monsters and mermaids.

Q Do mermaids really exist?

A Nobody really knows if mermaids exist, but it is unlikely. The manatee, a plant-eating marine mammal, may be the source of this famous legend. The female manatee floats upright while nursing her young, using her front feet to cradle it. From a distance, this might look like a human mother with her baby in her arms.

Q Where is the lost island of Atlantis supposed to be?

A Legend has it that the beautiful island of Atlantis sunk without a trace with all its inhabitants after a massive volcanic eruption. It has never been found, but some believe it is under the sea near the Greek or Canary Islands.

Q What was the *Marie Celeste*?

A The *Marie Celeste* was a large ship which was found on 3 December 1872 drifting in the Atlantic Ocean. Mysteriously, all of the crew had completely vanished, leaving their breakfasts half-eaten on the table! To this day no clues to the crew's whereabouts have been found.

Q What is the Bermuda Triangle?

A The Bermuda Triangle is a large area of the Atlantic Ocean that stretches between Bermuda, Puerto Rico and Florida where ships and aircraft have mysteriously gone missing without a trace. Some people believe that they have been kidnapped by UFOs!

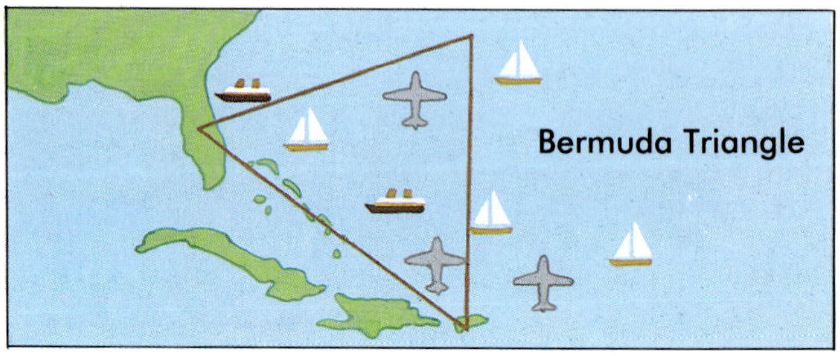

The giant squid has the biggest eyes of any animal. They are 17 times bigger than human eyes, measuring 40 cm across.

Q Are there really sea monsters?

A There are many stories of krakens, huge octopus-like creatures, which could easily turn over a ship. This legend is probably based on the giant squid. Although they do not grow big enough to overturn a large ship, they can weigh up to two tonnes and measure 15 metres long!

Neptune

Q Who are the ocean gods?

A For thousands of years, many cultures across the world have worshipped sea gods and goddesses, hoping they will keep them safe on long journeys across the sea or bring them luck when fishing.

Q What is the *Flying Dutchman*?

A The *Flying Dutchman* is a famous ghost ship. The story has it that the ship left Amsterdam in the 17th century for the East Indies and ran into a fierce storm. Her captain, dared by a ghostly devil, sailed right into the storm wrecking his ship and killing everyone onboard. The ship and her crew continue to haunt the seas, bringing bad luck to all that see her.

An estimated 2 million seabirds and 10,000 marine mammals are killed each year due to human waste dumped into the sea.

How do we look after the sea?

The sea, like the land, is suffering badly from pollution. For many years the sea has been used as a dumping ground for a variety of human waste products, all of which can have harmful effects on the creatures that live there.

Q What are the main causes of sea pollution?

A There are five main causes of pollution to the sea:
1) Nuclear waste from power stations.
2) Rubbish and heavy metals from industry, like lead and mercury.
3) Chemicals washed from the land into rivers and the sea, like fertilizers and pesticides.
4) Oil from coastal industries, ships and tanker spillages.
5) Sewage pumped into the sea.

Q Why is Minamata Bay in Japan famous?

A Between 1953 and 1960 hundreds of villagers in Minamata Bay in Japan were poisoned and 649 people died. This is because they had eaten shellfish contaminated with mercury which had been dumped into the sea by local industries.

Q What is being done about pollution?

A Recently environmental groups like Greenpeace and some governments are promoting a new theory called 'clean production'. This means that scientists are designing production processes and products that have no, or very little, toxic waste and so will cause minimum damage to the environment.

Q What is sewage?

A Sewage is waste which comes from homes, offices, shops and factories. It is 99 per cent water but also contains lots of harmful chemicals like ammonia. The sewage is separated into solids and liquids and then pumped into the sea, causing terrible pollution in some areas.

Over 1 billion 365 million litres of sewage is dumped into our coastal waters every day, most of which is untreated.

Fifty per cent of the household rubbish families throw away is packaging, costing £362 million each year.

Q What can you do to help?

A You should think about waste and how to recycle it. Here are some things you can do:
1) Try not to buy goods with lots of wrapping.
2) Find out if your local council have a recycling station for paper, cans, bottles and clothes.
3) Cut down on electricity by turning off lights when you are not in a room.
4) Try walking or cycling short distances with your family instead of taking the car.

Q What sea creatures are in danger?

A Some sea creatures have already become extinct. Many more are in danger, such as those pictured in the panel opposite.

Q When was one of the largest oil tanker accidents?

A In March 1989 the massive oil tanker, the *Exxon Valdez*, ran aground in Alaska where it poured 45 million litres of oil into the sea. This killed an estimated 100,000 seabirds and hundreds of thousands of fish, seals and shellfish.

Forty years ago floods killed 1,400 people in the Netherlands, and 307 in England.

What is the sea's future?

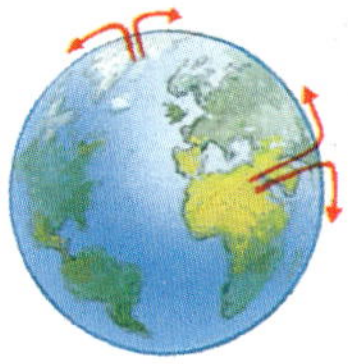

Temperatures around the world are gradually rising, known as global warming. This is having severe effects on the environment, including the sea.

Q What is the Greenhouse Effect?

A The Greenhouse Effect is the term used to describe how the Earth is kept warm by gases in the atmosphere trapping heat. Scientists believe that the Greenhouse Effect is increasing as more of the gases are being given off into the atmosphere.

Q Which gases are harmful?

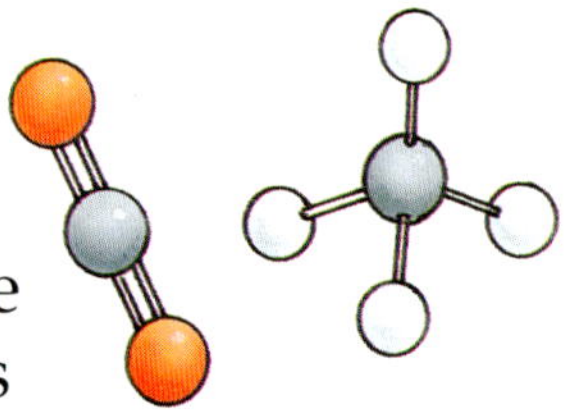

A Carbon dioxide and water vapour are the main greenhouse gases. Carbon dioxide is given off by power stations and factories. It is also given off as forests are burned to make way for farmland and building. Chlorofluorocarbons (CFCs) are given off by aerosol sprays and refrigerators. Nitrous oxides come from car exhaust fumes and from fertilizers. Methane is given off from rotting vegetation and rubbish.

Q What is an El Nino?

A An El Nino is a large, natural current which occurs about every 5 years in the Pacific Ocean. This current causes the sea level to fall, the water temperature to rise, torrential rain to fall and coral reefs to die. This is only a temporary disaster which gives us an example of what could happen worldwide if global warming continues.

When unusually warm waters entered the Galapagos coral reefs in 1983, more than 90 per cent of the corals died.

The sea temperature only has to increase by 2 or 3°C and all corals will die!

Q What is coral bleaching?

A Corals are the first to show signs of suffering when the sea temperature rises. It causes them to go completely white (to bleach!). Tiny plants called Zooxanthellae live inside them, providing their food and giving them their colour. As soon as the water gets warmer these tiny plants are expelled from the coral. At first the coral loses its colour, but eventually it will die.

Q Is the sea level rising?

A Many scientists believe that as temperatures are increasing (called global warming), the sea level is rising at an average rate of 1 to 2 mm per year. They think this is due to mountain glaciers melting.

Q What happens as the sea level rises?

A Rising water levels cause flooding, and this in turn causes erosion of the land. This can have disastrous consequences as more than 70 per cent of the world's population live on the coasts.

Q What will happen in the future?

A It is predicted that the sea level will rise by 3 to 10 mm each year in the future, if the temperature continues to increase at the present rate. Changes in the climate could mean an increase in violent storms with tsunamis and hurricanes causing coastal damage. Coastal cities under threat include Alexandria, Venice, Shanghai and London. Whole islands could disappear.

Index